Road to the Stanley Cup

The 2003-04 Calgary Flames' Unforgettable Season

Edited by Mike Bynum & Michelle White

The photos in the 1989 Calgary-Montreal game story are reprinted by permission of the Hockey Hall of Fame.

All other photos in this book are reprinted by permission of Rueters.

Reprinted by permission. The Calgary Flames game stories are edited versions of original stories published in *USA Today*. Reprinted by permission.

Cover and book design: Monica Washington, Birmingham, Ala.
Published by: Canada Hockey LLC

Cup Crazy in Calgary

It had been seven long seasons since the Calgary Flames had been to the Stanley Cup playoffs and 15 years since Lanny McDonald, Doug Gilmour, Al MacInnis, Mike Vernon and the 1988-89 Flames won hockey's greatest prize. But with the 2003-04 Flames' winning journey through the Western Conference playoffs, they have become Canada's top team and their fans have celebrated each victory with great excitement.

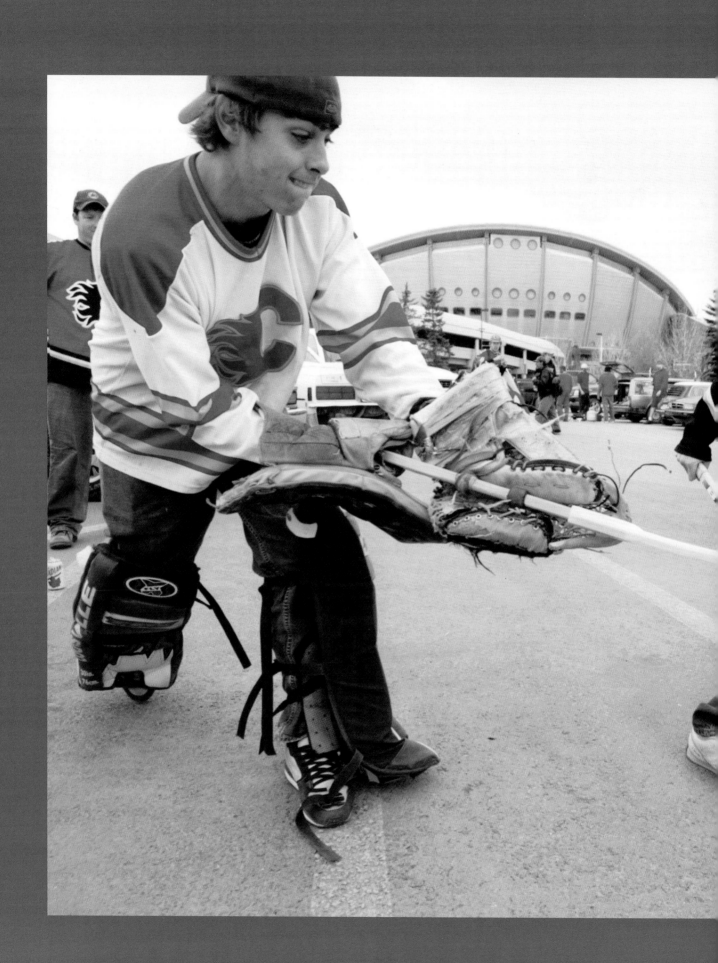

STANLEY CUP PLAYOFFS

Round 1

Calgary Flames vs. Vancouver Canucks

Oleg Saprykin (R) slaps the puck past Vancouver Canucks goalie Dan Cloutier during the second period.

Canuck's Power Play Defeats Calgary in Opener

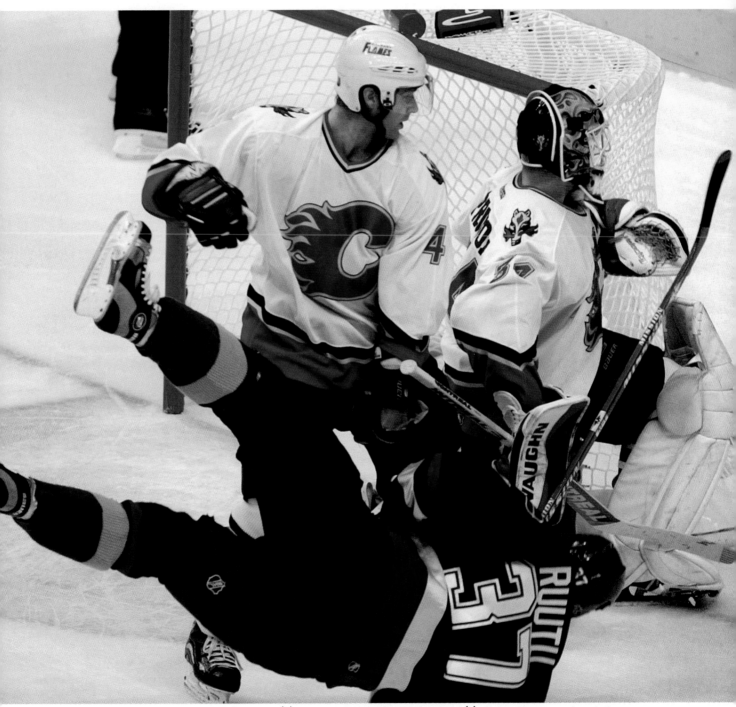

Jarkko Ruutu of the Vancouver Canucks (C) is uppended by Jordan Leopold (L) during the second period.

Game Summary

Calgary	0	2	1	—	3
Vancouver	2	2	1	—	5

FIRST PERIOD

Scoring: 1. Vancouver, Rucinsky 1 (Jovanovski, Naslund) 2:34 (power play). 2. Vancouver, Salo 1 (Morrison, Naslund) 5:24 (power play). Penalties — Nieminan, CAL (obstruction-hooking), 2:06; Nieminan, CAL (high-sticking), 4:34; Ruutu, VAN (holding the stick), 7:23; Cloutier, VAN (interference, served by Bergevin), 10:14; Simon, CAL (slashing), 15:51; Sanderson, VAN (goaltender interference), 17:23.

SECOND PERIOD

Scoring: 3. Calgary, Simon 1, 4:38 (power play). 4. Calgary, Saprykin 1 (Lombardi, Leopold) 5:06 (power play). 5. Vancouver, H. Sedin 1 (D. Sedin, Ohlund) 12:47 (power play). 6. Vancouver, Ohlund 1 (Morrison, Cooke) 17:51. Penalties — Donovan, CAL (obstruction-hooking), 0:36; Salo, VAN (interference), 3:10; Vancouver bench (too many men on ice, served by Sanderson), 4:32; Gelinas, CAL (obstruction-hooking), 11:02; Cooke, VAN (holding the stick), 12:59; Malik, VAN (cross-checking), 18:40.

THIRD PERIOD

Scoring: 7. VAN, Morrison 1 (Naslund, Jovanovski) 5:26 (power play). 8. CAL, Oliwa 1 (Leopold, Convoy) 6:16. Penalties: Nieminen, CAL (roughing), 5:17; Rucinsky, VAN (slashing), 7:40; Malik, VAN (obstruction-hooking), 12:53; Ohlund, VAN (high-sticking), 13:46.

Shots on Goal:

Calgary	4	12	13	—	29
Vancouver	6	10	8	—	22

Power-play Conversions: CAL - 2 of 10; VAN - 4 of 6.

Goalies: Kiprusoff (record: 0-1); Vancouver: Cloutier: (record 1-0).

Attendance: 18,630.

Referees: Eric Furlatt, Don Koharski.

Linesmen:

Ed Jovanovski of the Vancouver Canucks (R) is checked by Calgary Flames' Ville Nieminem during the first period.

Matt Cooke (24) is driven past the net by Flames' Denis Gauthier (3) as Flames' Miikka Kiprusoff covers up the puck.

Iginla & Kiprusoff
Lead Calgary Past Canucks

Vancouver Canucks' Ed Jovanovski (L) hits Calgary Flames' Matthew Lombardi during the first period.

Game Summary

Calgary	2	0	0	—	2
Vancouver	0	1	0	—	1

FIRST PERIOD
Scoring: 1, Calgary, Iginla 1 (Leopold, Simon), 3:06. 2, Calgary, Lombardi 1 (Unassisted), 3:56. Penalties: A Ference, Cgy (hooking), 5:37; Iginla, CAL (high sticking), 9:32; Morrison, VAN (holding), 13:50; Keane, VAN (obstruction hooking), 15:48.

SECOND PERIOD
Scoring: 3, Vancouver, Naslund 1 (power play) (Rucinsky, Salo), 9:41. Penalties: Malik, VAN (tripping), 3:10; Nilson, CAL (hooking), 7:50; Nieminen, CAL (delay of game), 8:53; Linden, VAN (high sticking), 9:03; Simon, CAL (diving), 16:52; Ohlund, VAN (hooking), 16:52; Ference, CAL (obstruction, hooking served by Kobasew), 19:32; Cooke, VAN (unsportsmanlike cond), 19:32.

THIRD PERIOD
Scoring: None. Penalties: Ohlund, Van (holding), 12:23; Lydman, CAL (high sticking), 16:54.

Shots on Goal:

Calgary	7	12	5	—	24
Vancouver	5	10	11	—	26

Power-play Conversions: CAL — 0 of 5, VAN — 1 of 5.
Goalies: Calgary, Kiprusoff (26 shots, 25 saves; record: 1-1-0). Vancouver, Cloutier (24 shots, 22 saves; record: 1-1-0).
Attendance: 18,630.
Referees: Don Van Massenhoven, Kerry Fraser.
Linesmen: Dan Schachte, Vaughan Rody.

Vancouver Canucks' Brent Sopel is roughed up by Calgary Flames' Jarome Iginla (12) during the third period.

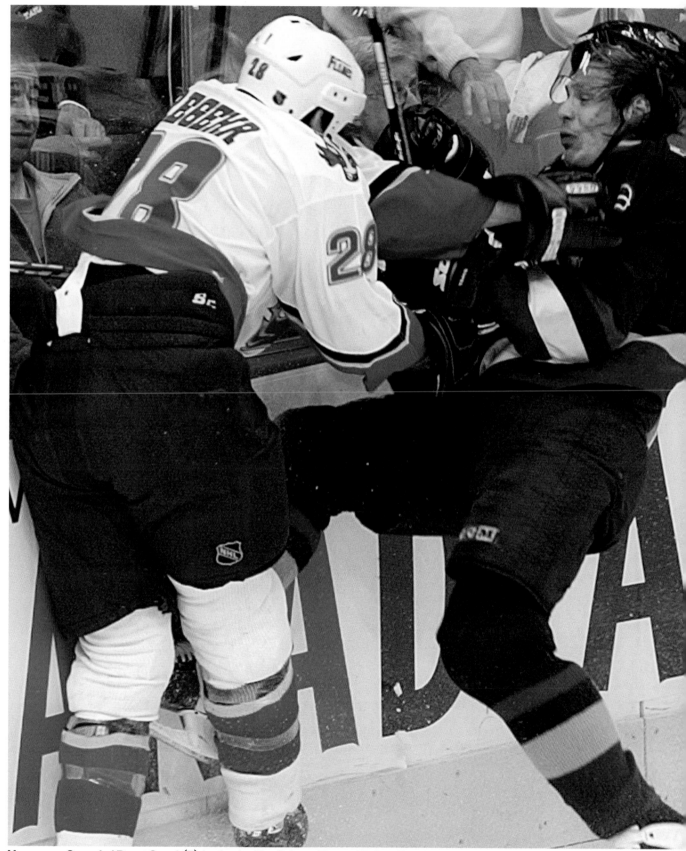

Vancouver Canucks' Brent Sopel (R) is checked by Calgary Flames' Robyn Regehr during the first period.

Calgary Flames forward Jarome Iginla (R) hits Vancouver Canucks forward Mike Keane in the first period.

Canucks Lose Cloutier, But Hedberg Holds Off Flames

Martin Gelinas (C) is knocked down by Canucks defenceman Sami Salo (R) in front of goalie Johan Hedberg.

Canucks goalie Dan Cloutier chats with referee Dan Marouelli after Cloutier injured himself and had to be replaced late in the first period.

Game Summary

Vancouver	0 1 1 — 2
Calgary	0 1 0 — 1

FIRST PERIOD
Scoring: None. Penalties: Nilson, CAL (holding stick), 5:38; Malik, VAN (double minor high sticking), 8:53; Simon, CAL (boarding), 9:58; Bergevin, VAN (holding), 15:38.

SECOND PERIOD
Scoring: 1, Calgary, Simon 2 (Lombardi, Iginla), 1:04. 2, Vancouver, Naslund 2 (power play) (Jovanovski), 2:10. Penalties: Lombardi, CAL (holding), 1:22; Rucinsky, VAN (high sticking), 6:51; Clark, CAL (slashing), 8:53; Naslund, VAN (hooking), 9:57; Clark, CAL (high sticking), 12:25; Linden, Van (interference), 14:23.

THIRD PERIOD
Scoring: 3, Vancouver, Cooke 1 (Morrison), 1:29. Penalties: Morrison, Van (holding), 14:24; Simon, CAL (roughing), 15:24; Ruutu, Van (roughing), 15:24; Ohlund, VAN (major fighting), 19:48; Iginla, CAL (major fighting), 19:48.

Shots on Goal:

Vancouver	12 8 5 — 25
Calgary	11 10 10 — 31

Power-play Conversions: VAN — 1 of 4, CAL - 0 of 7.
Goalies: Vancouver, Cloutier (11 shots, 11 saves), Hedberg (19:30 of 1st period, 20, 19; record: 1-0-0). Calgary, Kiprusoff (25 shots, 23 saves; record: 1-2-0).
Attendance: 19,289.
Referees: Chris Rooney, Dan Marouelli.
Linesmen: Mark Pare, Ray Scapinello.

Jordan Leopold (L), Robyn Regehr (C) and Shawn Donovan celebrate after Donovan's goal in the second period.

Yelle & Clark Pound Vancouver in 4-0 Win

Craig Conroy (L) and Jarome Iginla (R) crash into Canucks defenceman Mattias Ohlund in the first period.

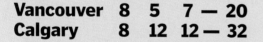

Game Summary

Vancouver	0	0	0	—	0
Calgary	0	3	1	—	4

FIRST PERIOD
Scoring: None. Penalties: Keane, VAN (tripping), 3:30; Nilson, CAL (cross checking), 6:56; Gelinas, CAL (slashing), 11:49; May, VAN (interference), 16:42; Donovan, CAL (high sticking), 19:28.

SECOND PERIOD
Scoring: 1, Calgary, Yelle 1 (shorthanded) (Clark), 0:58. 2, Calgary, Clark 1 (power play) (Gauthier, Kiprusoff), 16:06. 3, Calgary, Donovan 1 (Gelinas, Regehr), 16:33. Penalties: Morrison, VAN (goalie interference), 3:58; Yelle, CAL (hooking), 6:15; May, VAN (goalie interference), 8:43; H. Sedin, VAN (interference), 14:55; Gauthier, CAL (roughing), 17:06.

THIRD PERIOD
Scoring: 4, Calgary, Iginla 2 (empty net) (Unassisted), 18:13. Penalties: Conroy, CAL (goalie interference), 11:37; Jovanovski, VAN (slashing), 17:01; Regehr, CAL (high sticking), 17:34; Allen, VAN (goalie interference), 18:45; Commodore, CAL (cross checking), 18:45; Nieminen, CAL (roughing), 18:45.

Shots on Goal:

Vancouver	8	5	7	—	20
Calgary	8	12	12	—	32

Power-play Conversions: VAN — 0 of 8, CAL — 1 of 6.

Goalies: Vancouver, Hedberg (31 shots, 28 saves; record: 1-1-0). Calgary, Kiprusoff (20 shots, 20 saves; record: 2-2-0).
Attendance: 19,289.
Referees: Dean Warren, Stephen Walkom
Linesmen: Mark Pare, Ray Scapinello.

Ed Jovanovski (R) looks on as the puck flies by the hip of Calgary Flames goalie Mikka Kiprusoff in the first period.

Martin Gelinas of the Calgary Flames (R) celebrates the game winning goal by teammate Jarome Iginla.

Iginla's Third-Period Goal Gives Calgary a 2-1 Victory

Geoff Sanderson of the Vancouver Canucks (R) is stopped by Flames goalie Miikka Kiprusoff during the first period.

Game Summary

Calgary	0	1	1	— 2
Vancouver	0	1	0	— 1

FIRST PERIOD
Scoring: No Scoring. Penalties: Morrison, VAN (tripping), 4:12; Saprykin, CAL (roughing), 6:34; Clark, CAL (slashing), 8:35; Jovanovski, VAN (interference), 9:18; Iginla, CAL (roughing), 10:06; Donovan, Cal (holding), 14:57; Linden, VAN (holding), 19:37; Clark, CAL, Commodore, CAL (roughing), Ruutu, VAN (roughing, holding), 20:00.

SECOND PERIOD
Scoring: 1. Calgary, Conroy 1 (Commodore, Iginla) 3:50 (power play) 2. Vancouver, H.Sedin 2 (Salo, Ohlund) 16:19 (power play) Penalties: Gelinas, CAL (obstruction-interference), 0:28; Sanderson, VAN (obstruction-interference), 3:21; Clark, CAl (slashing), 15:25.

THIRD PERIOD
Scoring: 3. Calgary, Iginla 3 (Ference, Conroy) 5:37 Penalties: Gauthier, CAL (holding), 20:00.

Shots on Goal:

Calgary	8	10	2	— 20
Vancouver	8	13	12	— 33

Power-play Conversions: CAL — 1 of 3; VAN — 1 of 6.
Goalies: Calgary: Kiprusoff (record: 3-2); Vancouver: Auld (record: 0-1).
Attendance: 18,630.
Referees: Kevin Pollock, Rob Shick.
Linesmen: Lonnie Cameron, Mike Cvik.

Vancouver's Martin Rucinsky (L) checks Andrew Ference into the Canucks' bench, during the first period.

Vancouver Canucks forward Brendan Morrison celebrates his winning goal in the third overtime period.

Morrison's Goal Wins Wild 3-OT Thriller

Mikka Kiprusoff stops Vancouver Canucks forward Brad May (10) on a shot as Flames defenceman Robyn Regehr defends on the play in the first period.

Flames Stephane Yelle (L) and Vancouver Canucks forward Henrik Sedin (R) get tangled up in the second period.

Game Summary

Vancouver	1	3	0	0	0	1	—	5
Calgary	0	2	2	0	0	0	—	4

FIRST PERIOD
Scoring: 1, Vancouver, Ruutu 1 (H. Sedin, D. Sedin), 18:01.
Penalties: May, VAN (goalie interference), 0:44; Commodore, CAL (cross checking), 4:43; Oliwa, CAL (charging), 7:24; Yelle, CAL (holding), 12:26; Conroy, CAL (high sticking), 18:42.

SECOND PERIOD
Scoring: 2, Vancouver, D. Sedin 1 (power play) (Sopel, H. Sedin) 5:32. 3, Vancouver, May 1 (Sanderson, Chubarov),6:42. 4, Vancouver, Sanderson 1 (Ohlund, Naslund), 10:15. 5, Calgary, Saprykin 2 (Regehr, Conroy), 10:31. 6, Calgary, Nieminen 1 (Commodore), 12:38. Penalties: Yelle, CAL (interference), 4:31; Cooke, VAN (elbowing), 7:14; Rucinsky, VAN (high sticking), 17:43.

THIRD PERIOD
Scoring: 7, Calgary, Gelinas 1 (Clark, Regehr), 1:14. 8, Calgary, Chris Clark 2 (Regehr, Nilson), 12:56.

OVERTIME
Scoring: None. Penalties: Ohlund, VAN (holding), 19:24.

2ND OVERTIME
Scoring: None. Penalties: None.

3RD OVERTIME
Scoring: 9, Vancouver, Morrison 2 (Naslund), 2:28.

Shots on Goal:

Vancouver	15	9	9	10	7	2	—	52
Calgary	5	7	11	11	6	0	—	40

Power-play Conversions: VAN — 1 of 5, CAL — 0 of 4.
Goalies: Vancouver, Auld (40 shots, 36 saves; record: 1-1-0). Calgary, Kiprusoff (52 shots, 47 saves; record: 3-3-0).
Attendance: 19,289.
Referees: Dennis Larue, Mick Mcgeough.
Linesmen: Lonnie Cameron, Mark Wheler.

Calgary Flames goalie Mikka Kiprusoff looks into the net as Vancouver Canucks forward Daniel Sedin raises his arms as Geoff Sanderson congratulates him on a goal in the second period.

Jarome Inginla (L) celebrates after scoring his second goal against the Vancouver Canucks during third period.

Gelinas' Power-Play Goal Defeats Canucks in OT

Ville Nieminen of the Calgary Flames (L) checks Vancouver Canucks player Bryan Allen during the first period.

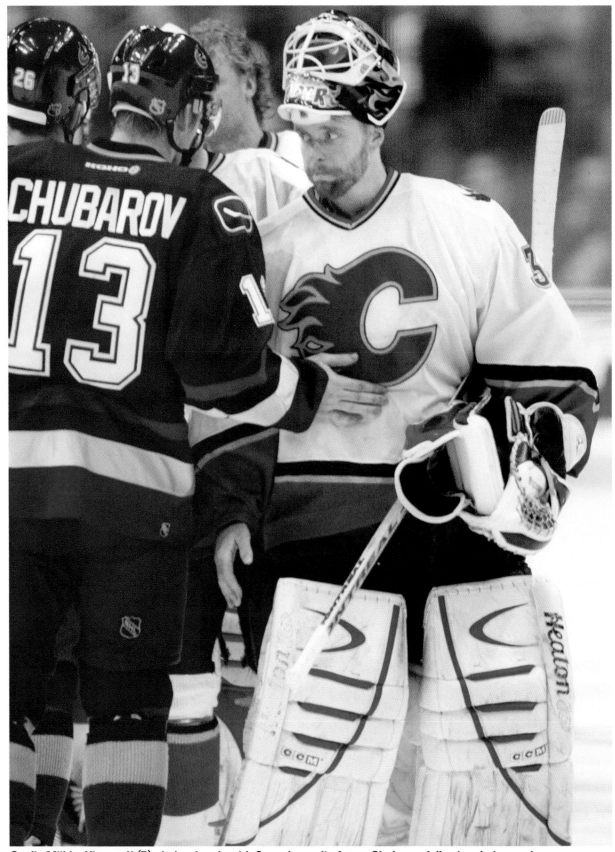

Goalie Miikka Kiprusoff (R) shakes hands with Canucks goalie Artem Chubarov following their overtime game.

Ville Nieminen (L) knocks Vancouver Canucks Bryan Allen into the boards head first during first period.

Jarome Iginla pushes the puck past Canucks goalie Alex Auld (L) and Sami Salo, during the third period.

Game Summary

Calgary	0	1	1	1	—	3
Vancouver	0	0	2	0	—	2

FIRST PERIOD
Scoring: None. Penalties: Nieminen, CAL (boarding), 7:09; Ruutu, VAN (roughing), 11:01.

SECOND PERIOD
Scoring: 1, Calgary, Iginla 4 (Conroy, Lombardi), 12:50. Penalties: Conroy, CAL (cross checking), 10:39; Cooke, VAN (goalie interference), 13:40; Montador, CAL (slashing), 17:16; Warrener, CAL (holding stick), 19:28.

THIRD PERIOD
Scoring: 2, Vancouver, Cooke 2 (Naslund, Jovanovski), 7:32. 3, Calgary, Iginla 5 (power play) (Leopold, Conroy) 10:14. 4, Vancouver, Cooke 3 (Naslund, Ohlund), 19:54 (with extra attacker). Penalties: Cooke, VAN (double minor high sticking), 9:34; Ference, CAL (slashing), 18:12; Jovanovski, VAN (high sticking), 19:33.

OVERTIME
Scoring: 5, Calgary, Gelinas 2 (power play) (Iginla, Yelle) 1:25.

Shots on Goal:

Calgary	6	6	13	3	—	28
Vancouver	7	10	11	0	—	28

Power-play Conversions: CAL — 2 of 5, VAN — 0 of 5.
Goalies: Calgary, Kiprusoff (28 shots, 26 saves; record: 4-3-0). Vancouver, Auld (28 shots, 25 saves; record: 1-2-0).
Attendance: 18,630.
Referees: Brad Watson, Dan Marouelli.
Linesmen: Brad Kovachik, Mark Wheler.

STANLEY CUP PLAYOFFS

Round 2

Calgary Flames vs. Detroit Red Wings

Flames Defeat Detroit, 2-1, in OT to Take Series Lead

Above: Red Wings' Kris Draper (C) is caught between Mike Commodore (2) and goalie Mikka Kiprusoff (34) in the first period. Left: Detroit's Derian Hatcher (C) gets checked into his goalie Curtis Joseph (R) by Ville Nieminen (L).

Game Summary

Calgary 0 1 0 1 — 2
Detroit 0 1 0 0 — 1

FIRST PERIOD
Scoring: No Scoring. Penalties: Draper DET (goaltender interference) 7:02, Oliwa CAL (obstruction-interference) 9:38.

SECOND PERIOD
Scoring: 1. Detroit, Lang 3 (Shanahan, Hatcher) 6:14; 2. Calgary, Regehr 1 (Lombardi) 17:57. Penalties: Nieminen, CAL (hooking), 1:41; Conroy, CAL (goaltender interference), 8:21; Zetterberg, DET (holding), 9:47; Shanahan, DET (hooking), 11:41; Gelinas, CAL (interference), 12:09; Kobasew, CAL (tripping), 14:58.

THIRD PERIOD
Scoring: No Scoring. Penalties: Yelle, Cal (high-sticking), 11:08.

OVERTIME
Scoring: 3. Calgary, Nilson 1 (Gelinas) 2:39. Penalties: None.

Shots on Goal:

Calgary 2 9 4 3 — 18
Detroit 13 9 6 1 — 29

Power-play Conversions: CAL — 0 of 3; DET — 0 of 6.
Goalies: Calgary: Kiprusoff (record 5-3-0); Detroit: Joseph (record 2-1-0).
Attendance: 20,066.
Referees: Marc Joannette, Don Van Massenhoven.
Linesmen: Ray Scapinello, Brian Murphy.

Red Wings leftwing Brendan Shanahan (14) and Calgary leftwing Ville Nieminen (24) watch as a shot by Wings Robert Lang (not in picture) scores against Flames goalie Mikka Kiprusoff in the second period.

Red Wings Rally for a 5-2 Win to Even Series

Detroit Red Wings Derian Hatcher (2) fights Calgary Flames Jarome Iginla (12) during the final minutes of Game 2.

Game Summary

Calgary	0 1 1 — 2
Detroit	0 3 2 — 5

FIRST PERIOD

Scoring: No Scoring. Penalties: Ference, CAL (holding), 1:21; Maltby, DET (tripping), 6:24; Kobasew, CAL (interference), 18:06.

SECOND PERIOD

Scoring: 1. Detroit, Holmstrom 2 (Lidstrom, Datsyuk) 3:02 (power play); 2. Detroit, Yzerman 2 (Dandenault, Lidstrom) 10:06; 3. Detroit, Yzerman 3 (Maltby, Draper) 12:19, 4. Calgary, Donovan 2 (Nilson) 13:50.
Penalties: Gelinas, CAL (goaltender interference), 1:40; Schneider, DET (roughing), 8:05; Kobasew, CAL (slashing), Holmstrom, DET (roughing), 13:19.

THIRD PERIOD

Scoring: 5. Detroit, Hull 3 (Lidstrom, Datsyuk) 14:49 (power play); 6. Detroit, Lidstrom 2 (Hull) 16:08 (power play); 7. Calgary, Gelinas 3, 18:50. Penalties: Donovan, CAL (slashing), 13:54; Commodore, CAL (slashing), 14:43; Regehr, CAL (cross-checking), 15:25; Chelios, DET (slashing), 16:42; Lombardi, CAL, Williams, DET (roughing), Shanahan, DET (charging), 19:20; Commodore, CAL, Iginla, CAL, McCarty, DET (fighting), Hatcher, DET (high-sticking, fighting) 19:36.

Shots on Goal:

Calgary	3 6 7 — 16
Detroit	15 11 6 — 32

Power-play Conversions: CAL — 0 of 5; DET — 3 of 6.
Goalies: Calgary: Kiprusoff (record: 5-4); Detroit: Joseph (record: 3-1).
Attendance: 20,066.
Referees: Dan Marouelli, Kevin Pollock.
Linesmen: Brian Murphy, Ray Scapinello.

Detroit Red Wings Steve Yzerman (19) scores his second goal against goalie Mikka Kiprusoff in the second period.

Calgary Flames Robin Regehr (R) holds Detroit Red Wings Henrik Zetterberg in a headlock during third period.

Donovan's Winning Goal Gives Flames a 2-1 Lead

Detroit Red Wings' goalie Curtis Joseph (R) stops a shot by Calgary Flames' Jarome Iginla during the first period.

Calgary Flames' goalie Mikka Kiprusoff (L) stops Detroit Red Wings' Henrik Zetterberg (R) during third period.

Game Summary

Detroit	0	2	0	—	2
Calgary	0	3	0	—	3

FIRST PERIOD
Scoring: None. Penalties: Dandenault, DET (interference), 4:58; Schneider, DET (high sticking), 8:53; Hatcher, DET (hooking), 13:22.

SECOND PERIOD
Scoring: 1, Detroit, Lang 4 (Mccarty, Shanahan), 1:17. 2, Calgary, Yelle 2 (Gelinas, Clark), 3:38. 3, Calgary, Iginla 6 (power play) (Gelinas, Lombardi), 5:46. 4, Detroit, Fischer 1 (Hull, Datsyuk), 11:44. 5, Calgary, Donovan 3 (Nilson, Nieminen), 12:24. Penalties: Fischer, DET (roughing), 4:47; Ference, CAL (roughing), 15:21.

THIRD PERIOD
Scoring: None. Penalties: Regehr, CAL (roughing), 3:14.

Shots on Goal:

Detroit	6	11	12	—	29
Calgary	10	12	5	—	27

Power-play Conversions: DET — 0 of 2, CAL — 1 of 4.
Goalies: Detroit, Joseph (27 shots, 24 saves; record: 3-2-0). Calgary, Kiprusoff (29 shots, 27 saves; record: 6-4-0).
Attendance: 19,289.
Referees: Bill Mccreary, Kelly Sutherland.
Linesmen: Dan Schachte, Mark Wheler.

Ville Nieminen (R) flips the puck over Detroit Red Wings goalie Curtis Joseph to tie the score during second period.

Dandenault & Wings
Even Series with 4-2 Win

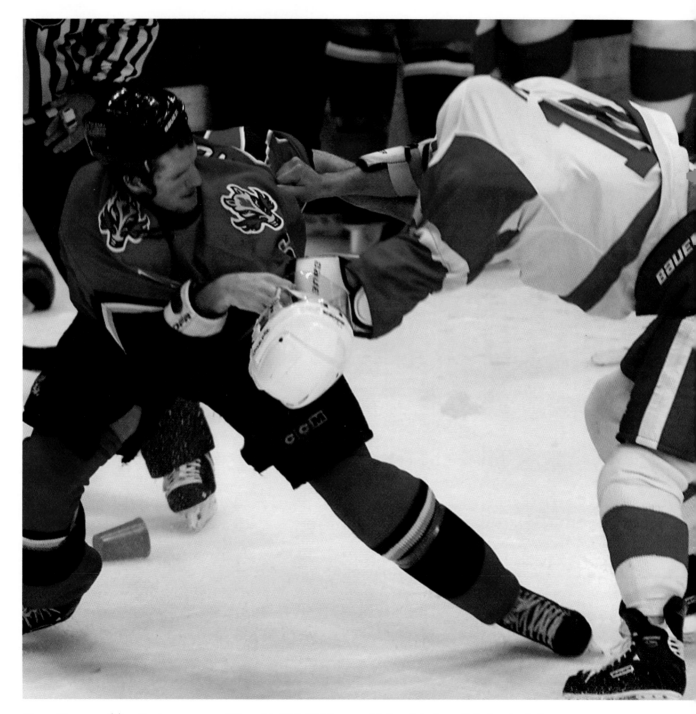

Shean Donovan (L) pulls the sweater of Detroit's Kirk Maltby over his head during a fight late in their game.

Detroit Red Wings Brett Hull (L) crashes into Calgary Flames goalie Mikka Kiprusoff during second period.

Game Summary

Detroit	1	1	2	—	4
Calgary	0	2	0	—	2

FIRST PERIOD
Scoring: 1, Detroit, Maltby 1 (Draper, Whitney), 0:26.
Penalties: Zetterberg, DET (holding), 13:29.

SECOND PERIOD
Scoring: 2, Detroit, Devereaux 1 (Whitney, Draper), 3:00. 3, Calgary, Gelinas 4 (Iginla, Conroy), 5:45. 4, Calgary, Nieminen 2 (Donovan, Nilson), 6:03.
Penalties: Lidstrom, DET (hooking), 13:20; Datsyuk, DET (cross checking), 19:49; Donovan, CAL (roughing), 19:49.

THIRD PERIOD
Scoring: 5, Detroit, Dandenault 1 (Holmstrom, Lang), 7:02. 6, Detroit, Zetterberg 2 (empty net) (Shanahan, Lidstrom), 19:36. Penalties: Regehr, CAL (roughing), 11:01; Shanahan, DET (roughing), 11:01; Donovan, CAL (major fighting), 19:56; Nieminen, CAL (major roughing, game misconduct), 19:56; Maltby, DET (major fighting), 19:56.

Shots on Goal:

Detroit	11	11	7	—	29
Calgary	9	11	7	—	27

Power-play Conversions: DET — 0 of 1, CAL — 0 of 2.
Goalies: Detroit, Joseph (27 shots, 25 saves; record: 4-2-0). Calgary, Kiprusoff (28 shots, 25 saves; record: 6-5-0).
Attendance: 19,289.
Referees: Dan O'Halloran, Stephen Walkom.
Linesmen: Dan Schachte, Mark Wheler

Oleg Saprykin (R) raises his arms as he celebrates teammate Craig Conroy's goal during the second period.

Conroy's 2nd Period Goal Defeats Red Wings

Craig Conroy (L) watches his shot get past Detroit goalie Curtis Joseph (C) in the second period.

Flames goalie Miikka Kiprusoff (L) makes a save against Detroit's Tomas Holmstrom (R) as he falls to the ice.

Game Summary

| Calgary | 0 | 1 | 0 | — | 1 |
| Detroit | 0 | 0 | 0 | — | 0 |

FIRST PERIOD
Scoring: No Scoring. Penalties: Fischer, DET (tripping), 2:23; Clark, CAL, Hatcher, DET (roughing) 3:53; Regehr, CAL (holding) 17:54.

SECOND PERIOD
Scoring: 1. Calgary, Conroy 2 (Iginla) 16:07. Penalties: Lang, DET (obstruction-hooking) 5:07, Leopold, CAL (holding), 5:42; Montador, CAL (slashing), 9:52; Commodore, CAL (boarding), 12:54.

THIRD PERIOD
Scoring: No Scoring. Penalties: Holmstrom, DET (roughing), 0:19, Ference, CAL (interference), 12:49.

Shots on Goal:

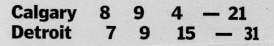

| Calgary | 8 | 9 | 4 | — | 21 |
| Detroit | 7 | 9 | 15 | — | 31 |

Power-play Conversions: CAL — 0 of 3; DET — 0 of 5.
Goalies: Calgary: Kiprusoff (record: 7-5-0); Detroit: Joseph (record: 4-3-0).
Attendance: 20,066.
Referees: Don Koharski, Kevin Pollock.
Linesmen: Paul Devorski, Brad Kovachik.

Detroit Red Wings' Pavel Datsyuk (L) takes Calgary Flames Roby Regehr into the boards during the first period.

Gelinas' OT Goal Wins Western Semi-Finals

Detroit's Curtis Joseph unsuccessfully dives (L) to try and stop Martin Gelinas (R) from scoring during OT.

Mikka Kiprusoff (L) stops the puck as Detroit's Kris Draper moves in for the rebound during the second period.

Calgary Flames Ville Nieminen (L) knocks Detroit Red Wings Mathieu Schmieder to the ice during the third period.

Game Summary

Detroit	0	0	0	0 —	1
Calgary	0	0	0	1 —	1

FIRST PERIOD
Scoring: None. Penalties: Maltby, DET (delay of game), 11:42; Rivers, DET (slashing), 13:59; Warrener, CAL (holding stick), 18:55.

SECOND PERIOD
Scoring: None. Penalties: Iginla, CAL (holding), 9:52; Maltby, DET (slashing), 14:09; Regehr, CAL (cross checking), 14:09.

THIRD PERIOD
Scoring: None. Penalties: Whitney, DET (obstruction-hooking), 1:33; Clark, CAL (tripping), 2:53; Lidstrom, DET (hooking), 10:51.

Shots on Goal:

Detroit	11	11	4	12 —	38
Calgary	11	9	13	11 —	44

Power-play Conversions: DET — 0 of 3, CAL — 0 of 4.

Goalies: Detroit, Joseph (44 shots, 43 saves; record: 4-4-0). Calgary, Kiprusoff (38 shots, 38 saves; record: 8-5-0).
Attendance: 19,289.
Referees: Don Van Massenhoven, Kerry Fraser.
Linesmen: Jean Morin, Ray Scapinello.

Calgary Flames Ville Nieminen (R) runs into Detroit Red Wings goalie Curtis Joseph during the first period.

1989 STANLEY CUP

Calgary Flames vs. Montreal Canadiens

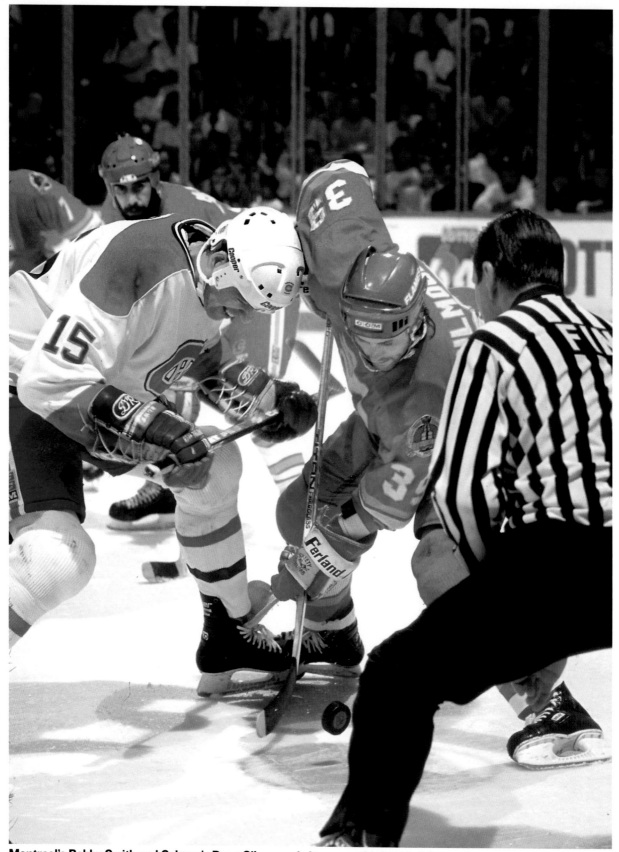

Montreal's Bobby Smith and Calgary's Doug Gilmour mix it up on a third-period face-off.

Flames Rule Canadiens' Forum for First Stanley Cup

Montreal Loses First Cup Finals on Home Ice

The Calgary Flames celebrated their first Stanley Cup tonight in unchartered territory, beating the Montreal Canadiens, 4-2, and taking the final series, four games to two.

It was the first time the Canadiens ever had ever watched as an opponent celebrated a Cup triumph at the Forum. For fans not used to such disappointment, the 17,909 in the Forum responded admirably, standing and clapping for the winners.

Lanny McDonald, the Flames captain, sent Calgary ahead to stay at 4:24 of the second period with his first goal of the playoffs. McDonald, 36, had not even dressed for the three previous games. At the end, he was presented the Cup along with co-captain Jim Peplinski, a scratch who came out in sweat clothes.

"I think you appreciate it a heck of a lot more after 16 years than after one or two," McDonald said. "This is the most peaceful feeling I've ever experienced in hockey. There's no feeling like it."

Doug Gilmour added the two clinching goals for the Flames, bringing his playoff total to 11, and said, "This is such an unbelievable city with so much tradition, you feel badly to break the streak here. But we're happy to win the Stanley Cup for ourselves."

Al MacInnis, extending his point-scoring streak to 17 games with two assists, won the Conn Smythe Trophy as the playoff MVP. MacInnis led all playoff scorers with 31 points, the first defenseman to finish on top in the postseason race.

"Right now I'm just on Cloud 9," MacInnis said. "We've been listening to mystiques about the Montreal Forum and the Canadiens since the series began, but we didn't pay much attention. We just wanted the

Stanley Cup, whether we were in the Spectrum or Madison Square Garden or here."

Calgary became only the fourth expansion team team to take the Cup, joining Philadelphia, the New York Islanders and Edmonton. The Flames entered the NHL in 1972, based in Atlanta, and not one member of the current club had played for a Stanley Cup champion.

The Flames wrapped up the Cup with three straight victories, scoring first in each of those games. Meanwhile, the Canadiens were losing three in a row for the first time this season.

Most of the goals were rather unusual, beginning with the opening score by Colin Patterson, Calgary's best checking forward, with 1:09 remaining in the first period.

Dana Murzyn dumped the puck toward the Montreal end and the puck caromed off defender Chris Chelios to Patterson, alone in the high slot. He lined it over the right pad of goalie Patrick Roy on the Flames' third shot of the period.

Stanley Cup Final

Game 1: Calgary 3, Montreal 2
Game 2: Montreal 4, Calgary 2
Game 3: Montreal 4, Calgary 3 (2OT)
Game 4: Calgary 4, Montreal 2
Game 5: Calgary 3, Montreal 2
Game 6: Calgary 4, Montreal 2

The Canadiens got that back on their first shot of the second period. Claude Lemieux croseed the blueline near the right-wing boards and fired a rising shot on which Calgary goalie Mike Vernon appeared to be tickled by the Forum ghosts everyone has been talking about.

Vernon, only 5 feet 9, raised both arms over his head and the puck struck his blocker, dropping behind him and trickling across the line.

After McDonald served a minor penalty for holding, he put the Flames in front to stay. Coming out of the box, he skated across the ice toward the Calgary bench, just as the Canadiens lost the puck while pressing for a score.

As Lemieux fell, Hakan Loob turned the play the other way, igniting a three-on-two with Joe Nieuwendyk and Jamie Macoun. All five players were on the left side of the ice and McDonald, seeing things develop, turned and found himself alone on the right side. He took Nieuwendyk's rinkside pass and beat Roy on the short side.

"I scored my first NHL goal in the Montreal Forum and this is a nice way to finish it off for now," McDonald said. "I'm not saying I'm ending it. I might just drop back and play defense for five more years."

A few minutes later, Shayne Corson bumped Vernon in a struggle for a rebound and Vernon punched him, giving Montreal a power play. The Canadiens came close three times, with Lemieux hitting a post, but they were unable to pull even.

"Mike Vernon is paid to stop the puck and we told him that after the first ruckus," said Flames coach Terry Crisp. "We told him just to pick himself up and leave the rest of it to his teammates."

Vernon picked himself up after he was flattened by Russ Courtnall in the third period and Calgary benefited when Courtnall was sent off for boarding.

It took only 16 seconds for Gilmour to bat in a midair rebound of his own backhander, for a 3-1 lead with 8:58 remaining to play. It was the Flames' seventh power-play goal of the series; Montreal had yielded only two in 15 playoff games against Hartford, Boston and Philadelphia.

Montreal got that back 51 seconds later on Rick Green's first playoff goal since the 1986 final series, in which Montreal defeated Calgary. Lemieux bumped Vernon off balance before Green's shot reached the net,

Game Summary

Calgary	1	1	2 —	4
Montreal	0	1	1 —	2

FIRST PERIOD
Scoring: 1, Calgary, Patterson 3 (Murzyn, MacInnis), 18:51. Penalties: Mullen, CAL (hooking), .54; Chelios, MON (elbowing), 5:09; Naslund, MON (interference), 8:20; M. Hunter, CAL (roughing), 9:53; Skrundland, MON (roughing), 9:53; Murzyn, CAL (tripping), 10:26; Roberts, CAL (roughing), 18:30; Ramage, CAL (roughing), 18:30; Corson, MON (roughing), 18:30; Smith, MON (roughing), 18:30.

SECOND PERIOD
Scoring: 2, Montreal, Lemieux 4 (Skrundland, Chelios), 1:23. 3, Calgary, McDonald 1 (nieuwendyk, Loob), 4:24. Penalties: McDonald, CAL (roughing, served by Roberts), 6:37; Loob, CAL (roughing), 6:37; Corson, MON (roughing), 6:37; Ludwig, MON (slashing), 11:08; Nattress, CAL (hooking), 16:36.

THIRD PERIOD
Scoring: 4, Calgary, Gilmour 10 (Otto, MacInnis), 11:02 (power play). 5, Montreal, Green 1 (McPhee, Lemieux), 11:53. 6, Calgary, Gilmour 11 (Mullen, Macoun), 18:57 (empty net). Penalties: M. Hunter, CAL (holding), 2:17; Skrundland, MON (roughing), 2:17; Courtnall, MON (boarding), 10:46; MacInnis, CAL (roughing), 18:34; Lemieux, MON (roughing minor misconduct), 18:34.

Shots on Goal:

Calgary	4	8	7 —	19
San Jose	9	7	6 —	22

Power-play Conversions: CAL -- 1 of 4; Mon -- 0 of 5.
Goalies: Calgary, Vernon, (22 shots, 20 saves; record: 16-5). Montreal, Roy (19 shots, 20 saves; record 13-6).
Attendance: 17,909.
Referees: Denis Morel.
Linesmen: Ron Finn, Swede Know.

In a post-game lockerroom celebration, **Calgary's Tim Hunter enjoys a sip of champagne from the Stanley Cup.**

but referee Denis Morel allowed it anyway.

Vernon was tripped from behind by Smith without a penalty. Then he stopped a shot by Mike McPhee and, when Lemieux overskated the rebound, the burly winger crashed into Vernon. Lemieux and MacInnis drew coincidental minors on that one.

Gilmour finally ended the suspense on an empty-net goal with 63 seconds left, leaving the Canadiens to bear the stigma of losing the Cup on home ice.

"Right now I feel empty inside," said center Ryan Walter, probably Montreal's best playoff performer. "The Flames were good at protecting the lead and that's our game. We would have liked to get the early lead and let them suffer a bit."

Vernon said, "We kept saying in the dressing room, 'Let's win this for Lanny.' After letting in the first goal, I was really frustrated, but Lanny came back and scored a big one for us. What could be more fitting?"

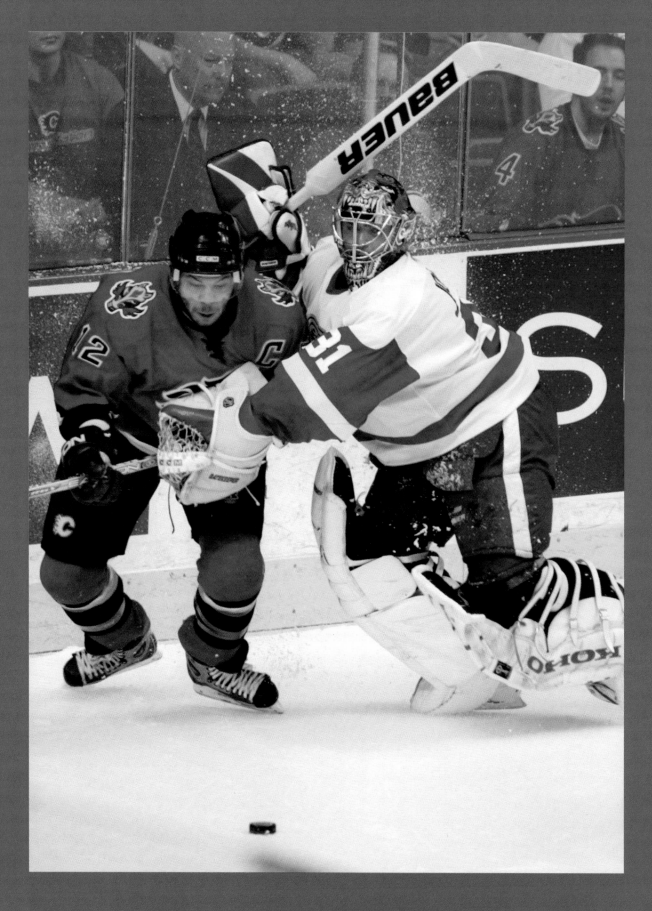

FLAMES HEROES & STATS

GOAL SCORING

NAME	TEAM	GP	G
Jarome Iginla	CGY	19	10
Vincent Lecavalier	TAM	15	9
Keith Primeau	PHI	17	9
Ruslan Fedotenko	TAM	15	8
Brad Richards	TAM	15	8
Patrick Marleau	SAN	17	8
Joe Sakic	COL	11	7
Vincent Damphousse	SAN	17	7
Joe Nieuwendyk	TOR	9	6
Alexei Kovalev	MON	11	6
Fredrik Modin	TAM	15	6
Martin Gelinas	CGY	19	6
Milan Hejduk	COL	11	5
Martin St. Louis	TAM	15	5
Simon Gagne	PHI	17	5
Michal Handzus	PHI	17	5
Alex Korolyuk	SAN	17	5
Craig Conroy	CGY	19	5

Jarome Iginla

INDIVIDUAL SCORING LEADERS

PLAYER	TEAM	GP	G	A	PTS
Jarome Iginla	CGY	19	10	7	17
Martin St. Louis	TAM	15	5	12	17
Keith Primeau	PHI	17	9	7	16
Brad Richards	TAM	15	8	7	15
Fredrik Modin	TAM	15	6	9	15
Craig Conroy	CGY	19	5	10	15
Vincent Damphousse	SAN	17	7	7	14
Alexei Zhamnov	PHI	17	4	10	14
Vincent Lecavalier	TAM	15	9	4	13
Jeremy Roenick	PHI	17	4	9	13
Patrick Marleau	SAN	17	8	4	12
Joe Sakic	COL	11	7	5	12
Martin Gelinas	CGY	19	6	6	12
Peter Forsberg	COL	11	4	7	11
Saku Koivu	MON	11	3	8	11

Martin Gelinas

2003-04 Playoffs Goalie Wins

RK	PLAYER	TEAM	GP	W
1	**Miikka Kiprusoff**	CAL	19	12
2	Nikolai Khabibulin	TAM	15	11
3	Robert Esche	PHI	17	11
4	Evgeni Nabokov	SAN	17	10
5	David Aebischer	COL	11	6

2003-04 Playoffs Goalie Shutouts

RK	PLAYER	TEAM	GP	SO
1	**Miikka Kiprusoff**	CAL	19	4
2	Nikolai Khabibulin	TAM	15	4
3	Evgeni Nabokov	SAN	17	3
4	Ed Belfour	TOR	13	3
5	Robert Esche	PHI	17	1

STANLEY CUP PLAYOFFS

Round 3

Calgary Flames vs. San Jose Sharks

Road Warrior Flames Bite Sharks in Overtime

Iglina & Co. Lead San Jose 1-0

BY ANDY GARDINER
USA TODAY

Calgary coach Darryl Sutter claims defenseman Steve Montador was slamming his stick so hard on the ice for the puck, you could hear him all the way to Sacramento. But Montador's demand paid off with the winning goal Sunday as the Flames topped the San Jose Sharks 4-3 in overtime in the Western Conference finals opener.

Montador took a pass just inside the blue line from Jarome Iginla on the left wing, skated in alone on goalie Evegni Nabokov and snapped a short shot home for the winner with 1:13 left in the extra period. It was Montador's first point in the playoffs and Calgary's fourth overtime win this postseason.

"I don't usually do that (banging his stick) because you don't want to give yourself away," said Montador, who had played in seven of the Flames' 13 previous playoff games but was thrust into extended action by injuries. "But I wanted to make sure Jarome heard me. I told him, 'Thanks for listening.'"

Montador's goal reversed an overtime dominated by San Jose. The Sharks outshot the Flames 12-5 and finished with a franchise-record 52 shots. But the Sharks were undone by what coach Ron Wilson called "a detail thing."

"It was a bad (line) change, and we didn't place the puck properly at the end of a shift," Wilson said. "They counterattacked and took adantage of probably the only mistake we made in overtime."

The game was every bit as close as expected between two teams with a long history of looking at the conference finals from the sideline. Calgary hadn't survived the opening round since winning the Stanley Cup in 1989. San Jose had never reached the third round in its 19-year history.

The Flames, who had three first-period goals in the previous two series, quieted the sellout crowd of 17,496 at HP Pavilion by taking a 2-0 lead against Nabokov, who came in with a 1.34 goals-against average and .949 save percentage. Fourth-line wing Krzysztof Oliwa scored midway through the period, and Craig Conroy connected with 31 seconds left.

Miikka Kiprusoff, who set a modern-day NHL record with a 1.69 goals-against average this season, stopped 18 San Jose shots in the first 20 minutes, including four during a two-minute 5-on-3 Sharks advantage.

"Say what you want, that's the difference right there," Sutter said.

The Sharks pulled even with goals from Mike Ricci and Todd Harvey in the second period, ending Kiprusoff's scoreless streak at 170 minutes, stretching back to Game 4 against Detroit.

Calgary regained the lead on Conroy's slap shot from the blue line with 9:25 gone in the third period that slipped just inside the right post. But the Sharks forced overtime when Alexander Korolyuk's shot from along the right boards deflected off a Calgary defender and knuckled over Kiprusoff's left shoulder with 3:21 to play.

Iginla, Calgary's playoff scoring leader with 12 points, did not manage a shot Sunday. The scoring came from

Steve Montador (5) is congratulated by Robyn Regehr (28) after scoring the game winning goal in overtime.

Goalie Evgeni Nabokov (20) is joined by Sharks defenseman Brad Stuart (7) and Flames' Shean Donovan (16) as they watch a shot by Flames defenseman Steve Montador go into the net for the game-winning goal in overtime.

unlikely sources, which pleased Sutter. "Monty scores for us, Oliwa scores for us, that's what we need," Sutter said.

Both teams stuck to the strategies that propelled them into this unlikely matchup of teams that missed the playoffs last season. San Jose rallied from 14th place in the conference last spring to the best season in franchise history, while the sixth-seeded Flames ended an eight-season playoff drought before upsetting Vancouver and Detroit.

"The bottom line is, I would bet it's easier to win the first game in this building than it would be Game 7," said Sutter, the Sharks' coach for five and a half seasons before getting fired in December 2002.

Notes: LW Scott Thornton returned to the Sharks lineup after missing five of the last seven playoff games with an undisclosed injury. ... Oliwa, who finished third in the league in penalty minutes, got his second goal of the playoffs. He had never scored an NHL postseason goal before this spring. ... Kiprusoff stopped 90 consecutive shots during a scoreless streak that included two 1-0 shutouts that finished off the Red Wings.

Game Summary

Calgary   2 0 1 1 — 4
San Jose 0 2 1 0 — 3

FIRST PERIOD
Scoring: 1, Calgary, Oliwa 2 (Saprykin, Kobasew),9:26. 2, Calgary, Conroy 3 (Donovan), 19:29. Penalties: Thornton, SJ (goalie interference), 4:17; Yelle, CAL (high sticking), 5:58; Simon, CAL (elbowing), 16:17; Clark, CAL (slashing), 16:17; Simon, CAL (roughing), 18:34; Mclaren, SJ (roughing), 18:34.

SECOND PERIOD
Scoring: 3, San Jose, Ricci 2 (Thornton, Cheechoo),1:23. 4, San Jose, Harvey 1 (Primeau, Hannan),19:02. Penalties: Nilson, CAL (charging), 20:00.

THIRD PERIOD
Scoring: 5, Calgary, Conroy 4 (Warrener, Leopold),9:25. 6, San Jose, Korolyuk 3 (Rathje, Mccauley),16:39. Penalties: Ekman, SJ (tripping), 5:48.

OVERTIME
Scoring: 7, Calgary, Montador 1 (Iginla, Donovan),18:43.

Shots on Goal:

Calgary   11   8 13   5 — 37
San Jose   18 15   7 12 — 52

Power-play Conversions: CAL — 0 of 2, SJ — 0 of 4.
Goalies: Calgary, Kiprusoff (52 shots, 49 saves; record: 9-5-0). San Jose, Nabokov (37 shots, 33 saves; record: 8-4-0).
Attendance: 17,496.
Referees: Kevin Pollock, Stephen Walkom.
Linesmen: Mark Wheler, Ray Scapinello.

Calgary Flames goalie Miikka Kiprusoff rubs his face while resting after a San Jose Sharks goal in the second period.

Above: San Jose's Alexander Korolyuk (L) and Flames defenseman Andrew Ference (R) struggle for the puck in front of supine Calgary goalie Miikka Kiprusoff in the second period. Below: Calgary Flames left wing Oleg Saprykin gets control of the puck as San Jose Sharks goalie Evgeni Nabokov watches in the first period.

Calgary Flames goalie Miikka Kiprusoff makes a save against San Jose Sharks' Curtis Brown during Game 2.

Flames Burning Bright After Shredding Sharks

Calgary Takes a 2-0 Western Conference Finals Lead

BY ANDY GARDINER
USA TODAY

The Calgary Flames rode a pair of first-period scores and two goals 44 seconds apart in the third period to a 4-1 victory against the San Jose Sharks Tuesday, giving them a stranglehold in the Western Conference final. The win was the second in a row for the Flames at HP Pavilion and gives them a 2-0 lead as the series shifts to the Saddledome in Calgary for Games 3 and 4 on Thursday and Sunday.

Calgary swept two regular-season games from the Sharks at home but are 3-3 at home in the playoffs. San Jose is 3-2 in playoff road games.

The Flames again made a first-period statement by bolting to a 2-0 lead for the second consecutive game. The San Jose crowd was still standing for the opening faceoff when Calgary struck 20 seconds into the game on Marcus Nilson's slap shot from the right faceoff circle that appeared headed wide until it caromed off the knee of Sharks defenseman Jason Marshall and past goalie Evgeni Nabokov.

The Flames made it 2-0 on only their third shot when Shean Donovan picked up a nifty drop pass from Ville Nieminen outside the San Jose blue line, skated in alone on Nabokov and tucked the puck inside the right post with 9:25 left.

The Sharks' frustration continued when they drew the first power-play chance of the game but then gave it back 18 seconds later when Vincent Damphousse was called for high sticking behind the Calgary net.

San Jose threw 18 shots at Flames goalie Miikka Kiprusoff in the first period of Game 1 but may not have touched the puck that many times in the opening 20 minutes Tuesday. The Sharks, outshot 8-4, never threatened.

But as it did in the opener, San Jose pulled itself back into the game during the second period. Alyn McCauley one-timed a slap shot from the left face-off circle for his first playoff goal with 5:26 gone, converting a backhand pass from behind the net from Nils Ekman. But the Sharks came up empty on two power-play chances and trailed 2-1 entering the final period.

After weathering early pressure from San Jose, Calgary put the game away in the third. Nieminen put a wrist shot through Sharks defender Scott Hannan that beat Nabokov to the stick side at 12:35. At 13:19, Flames captain Jarome Iginla, held to one shot in the opener, scored his seventh goal of the playoffs.

Calgary surrendered 52 shots in Sunday's 4-3 overtime victory but held San Jose to 18 in Game 2.

Western Conference Finals Series Record

Game 1: Calgary 4, San Jose 3 (OT)
Game 2: Calgary 4, San Jose 1
Game 3: San Jose at Calgary (May 13)
Game 4: San Jose at Calgary (May 16)
Game 5: Calgary at San Jose (TBA)
Game 6: San Jose at Calgary (TBA)

Game Summary

Calgary   2 0 2 — 4
San Jose   0 1 0 — 1

FIRST PERIOD
Scoring: 1, Calgary, Nilson 2 (Donovan, Montador), 0:20. 2, Calgary, Donovan 4 (Nieminen, Nilson), 10:35. Penalties: Clark, CAL (hooking), 11:41; Damphousse, SJ (high sticking), 11:59; Damphousse, SJ (tripping), 15:12; Saprykin, CAL (obstruction-hooking), 15:12.

SECOND PERIOD
Scoring: 3, San Jose, Mccauley 1 (Ekman, Davison), 5:26. Penalties: Simon, CAL (cross checking), 2:40; Dimitrakos, SJ (elbowing), 6:50; Simon, CAL (roughing), 14:53.

THIRD PERIOD
Scoring: 4, Calgary, Nieminen 3 (Unassisted), 12:35. 5, Calgary, Iginla 7 (Gelinas, Regehr), 13:19. Penalties: Damphousse, SJ (double minor roughing, high sticking), 17:01; Kobasew, CAL (slashing), 17:01.

Shots on Goal:

Calgary   8   6   6 — 20
San Jose   4   8   6 — 18

Power-play Conversions: CAL — 0 of 3, SJ — 0 of 3.
Goalies: Calgary, Kiprusoff (18 shots, 17 saves; record: 10-5-0). San Jose, Nabokov (20 shots, 16 saves; record: 8-5-0).
Attendance: 17,496.
Referees: Bill Mccreary, Don Van Massenhoven.
Linesmen: Mark Wheler, Ray Scapinello.

Calgary Flames' Shean Donovan (16) puts the puck past Sharks goalie Evgeni Nabokov for a first period goal.

Calgary Flames goalie Miikka Kiprusoff makes a glove save against the San Jose Sharks during Game 2.

San Jose Sharks' Mark Ricci is hit into boards by Calgary Flames Chris Simon.

Sharks goalie Evgeni Nabokov (R) makes a save on Flames winger Martin Gelinas (23) during the second period.

Visting Sharks Douse Red Hot Flames

Calgary Still Holds a 2-1 Lead in Series

BY ANDY GARDINER
USA TODAY

Home-ice advantage continued to be more of a curse than a blessing in the Western Conference final Thursday when the San Jose Sharks climbed back into the series by beating the Calgary Flames 3-0 at the Saddledome.

San Jose's victory cut Calgary's lead to 2-1 and extended the streak of the visiting team winning each game. Home teams have lost five of six games in the two conference finals.

Game 4 is Sunday afternoon at the 'Dome.

The newly formed line of Patrick Marleau, Vincent Damphousse and Alexander Korolyuk scored all of San Jose's goals.

It was a night of redemption for Sharks goalie Evgeni Nabokov. After allowing a total of seven goals in the semifinals against Colorado, he was torched for eight in the first two games against the Flames. But he was sharp from the opening faceoff and blanked Calgary with 34 saves for his third shutout of the postseason.

"We had some very good chances, but we didn't get enough traffic in front of Nabokov," Flames captain Jarome Iginla said. "We need to make it tougher on Sunday."

Backed by a deafening sellout crowd, the Flames hoped to shove the Sharks into a 3-0 hole only two teams in playoff history have overcome. Instead, second-seeded San Jose grabbed an almost must-win game.

No. 6 Calgary fell to 3-4 at home in the postseason.

"I hope it's not a lack of focus, because you want to be a tough team at home," Flames defenseman Rhett Warrener said. "They've been close losses, and that's playoff hockey."

The Sharks failed to score in the first period for the third consecutive game but at least came out with a scoreless tie instead of the 2-0 deficits they faced in Games 1 and 2. They were outshot 10-8 in the period, but Scott Thornton put a shot off the right post five minutes into play. Promising attempts from Curtis Brown midway through the period and Korolyuk in the final 10 seconds were thwarted by Flame goalie Miikka Kiprusoff.

San Jose's misery on the power play continued in the first, as the Sharks managed no shots on their first man advantage to go to 0-for-8 in the series.

"It was a typical road game for us in that we bend but don't break," Sharks coach Ron Wilson said. "We wanted to be aggressive and pressure when we could."

Wilson's juggled lineup paid off in the second period.

Defenseman Rob Davison sent a breakout pass from the Sharks' end to Korolyuk, who carried down the right wing. He fed a pass into the slot, and Damphousse put a backhander past Kiprusoff to finish a 3-on-2 break with 7:51 gone. It was Damphousse's sixth goal of the playoffs and San Jose's first lead in the series.

Calgary trailed for the first time since Game 4 of the semifinals against Detroit.

The Flames outshot the Sharks in every period (finishing with a 34-24 edge) and threw 14 shots at Nabokov in the final 20 minutes. But he stuffed everyone.

Korolyuk scored the clincher on a breakaway during a 4-on-4 situation in the final two minutes. Korolyuk

added an empty netter.

"(The line juggling) gave us a little more balance," Wilson said, "and (Korolyuk) was great, as he has been for most of the playoffs."

The Flames objected to the way Korolyuk took a measured shot into the empty net, and scuffles broke out.

"We're growing a dislike for them and I'm sure they're building one for us," said Iginla, who shaved his head for the game.

Left: Sharks left winger Alex Korolyuk (L) scores his team's second goal on Calgary Flames goaltender Miikka Kiprusoff during third period action in Game 3. Below: Miikka Kiprusoff stretches to stop a Sharks' shot in the second period.

San Jose Sharks goalie Evgeni Nabokov lands on Ville Nieminen (R) during third period in Game 3.

Game Summary

San Jose 0 1 2 — 3
Calgary 0 0 0 — 0

FIRST PERIOD

Scoring: None. Penalties: Mccauley, SJ (high sticking), 10:45; Yelle, CAL (interference), 16:31; Simon, CAL (holding), 19:50.

SECOND PERIOD

Scoring: 1, San Jose, Damphousse 6 (Korolyuk, Davison), 7:31. Penalties: Damphousse, SJ (elbowing), 9:01; Stuart, SJ (tripping), 14:30.

THIRD PERIOD

Scoring: 2, San Jose, Korolyuk 4 (Primeau), 18:10. 3, San Jose, Korolyuk 5 (power play) (Unassisted), 19:16. Penalties: Simon, CAL (), 6:16; Thornton, SJ (roughing), 6:16; Thornton, SJ (roughing), 16:53; Clark, CAL (roughing), 16:53; Nieminen, CAL (cross checking, served by Kobasew), 18:52; Simon, CAL (double instigator, served by Gelinas, roughing major, fighting, misconduct), 19:16;Rathje, SJ (major fighting), 19:16; Iginla, Cgy (unsportsmanlike conduct, misconduct, game misconduct), 19:16.

Shots on Goal:

San Jose 8 7 9 — 24
Calgary 10 10 14 — 34

Power-play Conversions: SJ -- 1 of 5, CAL -- 0 of 3.
Goalies: San Jose, Nabokov (34 shots, 34 saves; record: 9-5-0). Calgary, Kiprusoff (23 shots, 21 saves; record: 10-6-0).
Attendance: 19,289.
Referees: Brad Watson, Dan Marouelli.
Linesmen: Dan Schachte, Greg Devorski.

Calgary Flames Chris Clark (R) knocks San Jose Sharks' Jason Marshall during the first period.

Scrappy Sharks Prove They Still Have Bite

San Jose Evens Series at 2-2

By Andy Gardiner
USA TODAY

A series that has refused to follow form maintained its unpredictable nature Sunday. The San Jose Sharks' 4-2 victory against the Calgary Flames completed a weekend sweep that tied the Western Conference final 2-2. The road team not only hasn't lost in the series, it has never trailed. The Flames are 3-5 in postseason play at the Saddledome.

Game 5 is tonight in San Jose.

"It's back to square one," said Sharks coach Ron Wilson. "It's who scores first who wins. (Tonight) we have to make sure they don't get any sniffs and we get a good start."

The first period ended 0-0, meaning Calgary has not scored at home in the opening 20 minutes of any of its eight playoff games. San Jose seized control by scoring four times in the middle stanza.

Defenseman Mike Rathje, who suffered a black eye and three stitches in a dustup late in Game 3, exacted his revenge by rifling a rebound past Miikka Kiprusoff 2:40 into the period.

"This is the playoffs, and that kind of (goonery), it doesn't work," Rathje said. "We've had adversity all year, and we've kept going. That's not going to stop us." The Flames pulled even with 12:05 left in the period when Jarome Iginla's pass from behind the net wiggled through a scrum of bodies and slipped between Nabokov's pads.

But Jonathan Cheechoo caught Kiprusoff out of position 39 seconds later and tucked a shot into the corner from behind the net.

"It's always a big shift after (an opposing) goal," Cheechoo said. "We wanted to get the momentum back, and we got lucky."

Veteran Vincent Damphousse and rising star Patrick Marleau teamed for power play goals before the period ended to ensure a Game 6 in Calgary on Wednesday.

"We weathered a storm and had to kill a lot of penalties (three) in the first period," said Sharks defenseman Scott Hannan, who assisted on the first goal. "In the second period we had a good mind set, and the guys made big plays."

Kiprusoff was benched for the third period, the first time he has been off the ice in the playoffs.

"I think it was his weakest performance of the playoffs," said Calgary coach Darryl Sutter. "I thought we played a really good first period, and then we turned the puck over. We had so many turnovers it wouldn't have mattered where we played."

The Flames' Chris Simon scored with 40 seconds left, breaking Calgary's 0-for-24 streak on the power play. But the Flames needed a 5-on-3 advantage to do it. "They scored on their (power play) opportunities, and we didn't," Sutter said. "This game to me was a mirror of Game 2 (won by Calgary 4-1) except the opposite. The same concerns they had with their weak goals and defensive turnovers (are the concerns I have)."

"This one is behind us," Iginla said. "It's a best-of-three series now, and we've won both of our best-of-

threes this season. We've always found a way to get out of this, and we'll try to do it again."

Notes: Calgary's power play is 1-for-16 in the conference finals after failing to score in the final three games of the second round against Detroit. ... With Nils Ekman back in the lineup after a one-game absence, the Sharks scratched rookie RW Niko Dimitrakos, who spent most of the season on their top line. ... The Flames scratched tough guy Krzysztof Oliwa and activated former Sharks LW Dave Lowry, who appeared in just two previous playoff games.

San Jose's Mike Ricci (R) tries to get the puck past Flames goalie Miikka Kiprusoff (L) during first period.

Sharks Vincent Damphousse and Scott Hannan (L) celebrate after Damphousse scored during the second period.

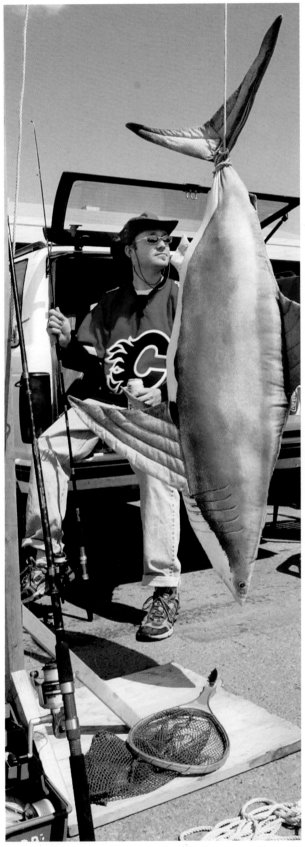

With fishing gear and rods included Flames fan Ryan Kaye displays a toy shark outside the Saddledome.

Game Summary

San Jose	0	4	0 —	**4**
Calgary	0	1	1 —	**2**

FIRST PERIOD

Scoring: None. Penalties: Donovan, CAL (high sticking), 4:52; Lowry, CAL (roughing), 7:19; Hannan, SJ (roughing), 7:19; Marleau, SJ (roughing), 8:18; Marshall, SJ (interference), 12:12; Nabokov, SJ (interference, served by Korolyuk), 17:30.

SECOND PERIOD

Scoring: 1, San Jose, Rathje 1 (Unassisted), 2:40. 2, Calgary, Iginla 8 (Gelinas, Conroy), 7:55. 3, San Jose, Cheechoo 4 (Unassisted), 8:34. 4, San Jose, Damphousse 7 (power play) (Marleau, Stuart), 10:03. 5, San Jose, Marleau 8 (power play) (Damphousse), 18:47. Penalties: Marshall, SJ (roughing), 4:16; Simon, CAL (roughing), 8:44; Leopold, CAL (high sticking), 11:17; Simon, CAL (interference), 15:19; Nieminen, CAL (major fighting), 18:19; Marshall, SJ (major fighting), 19:18.

THIRD PERIOD

Scoring: 6, Calgary, Simon 3 (power play) (Nilson, Leopold), 19:20. Penalties: Nilson, CAL (roughing), 6:22; Damphousse, SJ (roughing), 6:22; Ekman, SJ (high sticking), 7:29; Korolyuk, SJ (roughing), 9:23; Nilson, CAL (holding), 13:39; Marshall, SJ (roughing), 17:37; Davison, SJ (cross checking), 18:14; Mclaren, SJ (roughing), 19:52; Saprykin, CAL (roughing), 19:52; Simon, CAL (misconduct), 19:52; Thornton, SJ (misconduct), 19:52; Iginla, CAL (unsportsmanlike cond), 19:52.

Shots on Goal:

San Jose	6	10	3 —	**19**
Calgary	4	9	16 —	**29**

Power-play Conversions: San Jose, Nabokov (29 shots, 27 saves; record: 10-5-0). Calgary, Kiprusoff (16 shots, 12 saves; record: 10-7-0), Turek (start of 3rd period, 3, 3).
Attendance: 19,289.
Referees: Don Koharski, Marc Joannette.
Linesmen: Dan Schachte, Greg Devorski.

Goalie Evgeni Nabokov falls to the ice as Jarome Iginla (12) puts the puck by him for a score in the first period.

Flames on Cusp of Cup Berth

Calgary Moves Ahead With 3-2 Advantage

BY ANDY GARDINER
USA TODAY

The Calgary Flames might have turned into under-achievers at home this postseason, but their ability to win on the road has brought them within one game of the Stanley Cup Finals.

Calgary blitzed the San Jose Sharks 3-0 Monday to take a 3-2 lead in the Western Conference final. It was the sixth-seeded Flames' third consecutive win at the HP Pavilion and lifted their playoff road record to 8-2. That has offset a 3-5 record at the Saddledome and gives them a chance to close out the series at home Wednesday. The visiting team has won every game in the series.

"It's definitely different, what we're doing this year," said Iginla, who leads the NHL with 16 postseason points. "I can't put my finger on why it's working out this way. I don't think anybody can. It's kind of fun, though."

Second-seeded San Jose recovered after starting the series 0-2 by sweeping two games in Calgary, evening the series with a dominating 4-2 victory Sunday. But faced with an opportunity to seize control, the Sharks responded with a hideous first 20 minutes of turnovers, missed assignments and wayward passes.

"We didn't play hard, and I can't explain that," center Vincent Damphousse said. "We've been battling the odds ever since the beginning of the series, and we'll try

Nils Ekman and Niko Dimitrakos (L) try and screen Calgary Flames goalie Miikka Kiprusoff as the puck hits Ekman in the back during the first period.

to do it again. There's a lot of things we can do better. We just have to keep winning road games. That seems to be the trend."

The result was a 2-0 Calgary lead, the third consecutive time the Flames left the first period with a two-goal cushion at the Shark Tank. That was more than enough margin for Calgary goalie Miikka Kiprusoff. He had allowed four or more goals four times during the season and followed each loss with a victory, never allowing more than two goals.

Sharks coach Ron Wilson talked after Game 4 of the importance of a fast start in Game 5, because the team that scored first had won each of the previous four games. But after five minutes, the shots were 6-0 for the Flames, and San Jose was already stumbling.

"Where that performance came from, I really have no idea," Wilson said after Game 5. "It wasn't one or two guys. It was almost the whole team struggling. You have to give Calgary some credit, but we really did a pretty good job of shooting ourselves in the foot with some very elementary mistakes."

Calgary took the lead at 13:33 on the first short-handed goal of the series. Jarome Iginla intercepted a blue-line pass from Damphousse to Kyle McLaren and skated in on a breakaway. His offspeed shot slid past Evgeni Nabokov for a 1-0 lead and his playoff-best ninth goal.

That margin doubled two minutes later when Niko Dimitrakos' pass was picked off by Ville Nieminen, who passed across to Marcus Nilson. He ripped a slap shot past Nabokov from high in the slot. The Flames outshot the Sharks 12-6 in the period and held San Jose scoreless in the first for the fifth consecutive game.

The second period had been San Jose's best in the playoffs, producing a 19-5 goal advantage. And the Sharks pressured Kiprusoff by outshooting Calgary 9-4 in the period. But another defensive breakdown allowed Craig Conroy to skate in unmolested from the blue line and lift a shot into the upper right corner for a 3-0 lead with 7:13 remaining in the period.

There was no magical comeback in the third period for San Jose as it lost for the fourth consecutive time at home stretching back to the semifinal series against Colorado. Kiprusoff finished with 19 saves to earn his fourth shutout of the postseason and send the Sharks off to a chorus of boos from the sellout crowd of 17,496.

Kiprusoff, who was pulled before the third period of Game 4, was barely tested by the sleepwalking Sharks.

"Things change fast here," Kiprusoff said. "It's never fun when they pull you, but when I got pulled, I was already thinking about today's game."

Calgary has won the fifth game in all three of its series, first against the No. 3 Vancouver Canucks in the opening round and then against the No. 1 Detroit Red Wings in the semifinals.

San Jose Sharks Nils Ekman (R) hits Calgary Flames goalie Miikka Kiprusoff during Game 5.

Calgary Flames goalie Miikka Kiprusoff makes a save against the San Jose Sharks during Game 5.

Game Summary

Calgary	2	1	0	—	**3**
San Jose	0	0	0	—	**0**

FIRST PERIOD
Scoring: 1, Calgary, Jarome Iginla 9 (shorthanded) (Unassisted), 6:27. 2, Calgary, Marcus Nilson 3 (Ville Nieminen), 8:29. Penalties: Commodore, CAL (holding), 6:03; Hannan, SJ (obstruction-interference), 12:18; Montador, CAL (hooking), 16:38.

SECOND PERIOD
Scoring: 3, Calgary, Craig Conroy 5 (Unassisted), 12:47. Penalties: Davison, SJ (hooking), 5:27; Gelinas, CAL (hooking), 14:54; Gelinas, CAl (cross checking), 18:59.

THIRD PERIOD
Scoring: None. Penalties: Harvey, SJ (cross checking), 9:09.

Shots on Goal:

Calgary	12	4	5	—	**21**
San Jose	6	9	4	—	**19**

Power-play Conversions: CAL — of 3, SJ — 0 of 4.
Attendance: 17,496.
Referees: Brad Watson, Kerry Fraser.
Linesmen: Mark Wheler, Ray Scapinello.

Flames goalie Miikka Kiprusoff is cheered by fans after the Flames defeated the San Jose Sharks 3-1 in Game 6.

Flames Defeat San Jose to Reach Cup Finals

First Win on Home Ice in Series Clinches Berth

BY ANDY GARDINER
USA TODAY

The Calgary Flames finally won a Western Conference final game at the Pengrowth Saddledome, and it earned them their first trip to the Stanley Cup Finals in 15 years.

The sixth-seeded Flames beat the San Jose Sharks 3-1 Wednesday night in Game 6 for the first victory by the home team in the series. The Flames completed a play-off run past the three top-seeded teams in the conference. They'll open on the road Tuesday against the winner of the Philadelphia Flyers-Tampa Bay Lightning series.

Goalie Miikka Kiprusoff, obtained from San Jose in a November trade, made 18 saves and fended off a desperate Sharks attack in the third period.

One pattern continued and one ended in the first period. San Jose failed to score in the opening 20 minutes for the sixth consecutive game, but Calgary scored its initial first-period goal in nine postseason home games.

Jarome Iginla again was the man who pulled the trigger. Working with the period's only power play, he took a blue-line feed from Craig Conroy and wristed a shot past Evgeni Nabokov from the left faceoff circle for his playoff-leading 10th goal with 1:08 remaining.

That score capped a period in which Calgary outshot San Jose 11-6 and carried the play from the opening faceoff. The Sharks did not manage a shot for the first 5:35 and were forced to defuse a steady stream of offensive thrusts from the Flames.

The red-clad crowd of 19,289 took the noise at the Saddledome up another level when Martin Gelinas made it 2-0 with a goal with 13:02 gone in the second period. Conroy won a center-ice faceoff from Marcel Goc and fed Gelinas, who beat Nabokov with a wrist shot between the pads after faking a slap shot.

For Gelinas, who is known as "The Eliminator," it proved to be his third series-clinching goal of this post-season.

"Overall, it's just been a great team effort and everybody's been chipping in," he said. "It just happened that I'm in the right place at the right time."

But San Jose answered with Alyn McCauley's shot from the slot with 3:46 left in the period, converting a pass from Nils Ekman and beating Kiprusoff to the stick side.

That was all Kiprusoff allowed. The Sharks outshot the Flames 7-4 but came up with nothing.

Calgary had missed the playoffs the previous seven years. It now advances to the Finals for only the third time in history: The Flames won it all in their previous appearance in 1989.

"You never know when this opportunity is going to come again in your life," said Iginla, who leads the playoffs with 17 points. "You'd like to think it's going to happen every year ... but we know that's not the case. You have to grab it when it comes."

Calgary coach Darryl Sutter liked the symmetry attached to the Flames scoring.

"It was fitting that Jarome scores the first goal, the big goal, and Marty gets the winner," Flames coach Darryl Sutter said. "That's how our playoffs have gone."

Notes: The Canadian anthem will be sung in the Finals for the first time since Vancouver made it in 1994.

San Jose Sharks goaltender Evgeni Nabokov makes a
save on Calgary Flames Jarome Iginla (R) in Game 6.

Calgary Flames captain Jarome Iginla (R) accepts the Clarence Campbell trophy from the NHL's Bill Daly after winning the **NHL Western Conference final.**

Above: San Jose Sharks defenceman Scott Hannan (L) checks Calgary Flames right winger Jarome Iginla during first period. Below: Sharks' Kyle McLaren (L) punches Flames right winger Jarome Iginla during first period.

Game Summary

San Jose	0	1	0	—	1
Calgary	1	1	1	—	2

FIRST PERIOD
Scoring: 1, Calgary, Iginla 10 (power play) (Conroy, Leopold), 18:52. Penalties: C Brown, SJ (double minor high sticking), 18:27.

SECOND PERIOD
Scoring: 2, Calgary, Gelinas 6 Conroy), 13:02. 3, San Jose, Alyn Mccauley 2 (Nils Ekman, Mike Rathje), 16:14.
Penalties: O Saprykin, CAL (obstruction-interference), 4:40; Marshall, SJ (holding), 7:03; Mclaren, SJ (tripping), 9:42; Clark, CAL (interference), 17:16.

THIRD PERIOD
Scoring: 4, Calgary, Regehr 2 (empty net) (Unassisted), 19:59. Penalties: Regehr, CAL (hooking), 7:15.

Shots on Goal:

San Jose	6	6	7	—	19
Calgary	11	13	5	—	29

Power-play Conversions: SJ - 0 of 3, CAL - 1 of 4.
Attendance: 19,289.
Referees: Bill Mccreary, Kevin Pollock.
Linesmen: Greg Devorski, Ray Scapinello.

(Left to right) Dave Lowry, Jarome Iginla, Miikka Kiprusoff, Chris Simon and Jordan Leopold celebrate their win over the San Jose Sharks in Game 6 of their NHL Western Conference final.

The Calgary Flames celebrate their 3-1 win over the San Jose Sharks in Game 6.

Goalie Miikka Kiprusoff (R) hugs teammate Rhett Warrener as the Flames defeat the San Jose Sharks 3-1.

Calgary Flames Playoff History

Overall Playoff Record: 81-94
Stanley Cup Championships: 1988-89

2004 – defeated Vancouver, 4-3, Western Conference quarterfinals; defeated Detroit, 4-2, Western Conference semifinals; defeated San Jose, 4-2, Western Conference finals

1996 – lost to Chicago, 4-0, Western Conference quarterfinals

1995 – lost to San Jose, 4-3, Western Conference quarterfinals

1994 – lost to Vancouver, 4-3, Western Conference quarterfinals

1993 – lost to Los Angeles, 4-2, Smythe Division semifinals

1991 – lost to Edmonton, 4-3, Smythe Division semifinals

1990 – ost to Los Angeles, 4-2, Smythe Division semifinals

1989 – defeated Vancouver, 4-3, Smythe Division semifinals; defeated Los Angeles, 4-0, Smythe Division finals; defeated Chicago, 4-1, Campbell Conference finals; defeated Montreal, 4-2, Stanley Cup Finals

1988 – defeated Los Angeles, 4-1, Smythe Division semifinals; lost to Edmonton, 4-0, Smythe Division finals

1987 – lost to Winnipeg, 4-2, Smythe Division semifinals

1986 – defeated Winnipeg, 3-0, Smythe Division semifinals; defeated Edmonton, 4-3, Smythe Division finals; defeated St. Louis, 4-3, Campbell Conference finals; lost to Montreal, 4-1, Stanley Cup Finals

1985 – lost to Winnipeg, 3-1, Smythe Division semi-finals

1984 – defeated Vancouver, 3-1, Smythe Division semifinals; lost to Edmonton, 4-3, Smythe Division finals

1983 – defeated Vancouver, 3-1, Smythe Division semifinals; lost to Edmonton, 4-1, Smythe Division finals

1982 – lost to Vancouver, 3-0, Smythe Division semifinals

1981 – defeated Chicago, 3-0, preliminary round; defeated Philadelphia, 4-3, quarterfinals; lost to Minnesota, 4-2, semifinals

Jarome Iginla (L) and Martin Gelinas celebrate the win over the San Jose Sharks in Game 6.

Date	Opponent	Result	Score
Oct. 9	Vancouver	Loss	4-1
Oct. 11	Calgary	Win	3-2
Oct. 14	Edmonton	Win	1-0
Oct. 18	Buffalo	Loss	2-0
Oct. 21	Minnesota	Win	3-2
Oct. 24	St. Louis	Loss	2-1
Oct. 25	Edmonton	Win	4-2
Oct. 28	Colorado	Loss	4-2
Oct. 29	Dallas	Loss	4-3 (OT)
Nov. 1	Columbus	Win	3-0
Nov. 4	Detroit	Loss	3-0
Nov. 7	Minnesota	Loss	3-0
Nov. 9	Columbus	Loss	4-3
Nov. 12	Chicago	Win	6-2
Nov. 13	Nashville	Loss	4-1
Nov. 15	Edmonton	Loss	2-1 (OT)
Nov. 18	Toronto	Win	3-2 (OT)
Nov. 20	Montreal	Win	2-1
Nov. 22	Chicago	Win	2-1
Nov. 27	Colorado	Loss	6-5 (OT)
Nov. 29	Vancouver	Tie	4-4 (OT)
Dec. 2	San Jose	Win	3-1
Dec. 4	Vancouver	Win	4-1
Dec. 5	Minnesota	Win	2-1
Dec. 7	Pittsburgh	Win	6-1
Dec. 9	Minnesota	Loss	2-1
Dec. 11	Carolina	Win	1-0
Dec. 13	Colorado	Tie	1-1 (OT)
Dec. 16	Philadelphia	Win	3-2 (OT)
Dec. 18	Boston	Win	5-0
Dec. 19	Columbus	Win	2-1
Dec. 23	Edmonton	Win	2-1
Dec. 26	Vancouver	Loss	2-0
Dec. 28	Edmonton	Win	2-1
Dec. 29	Minnesota	Tie	2-2 (OT)
Dec. 31	Colorado	Loss	2-1
Jan. 3	Vancouver	Loss	3-1
Jan. 5	NY Rangers	Win	5-0
Jan. 6	NY Islanders	Win	3-2
Jan. 8	Chicago	Loss	3-1
Jan. 10	Florida	Win	4-2
Jan. 13	Toronto	Loss	4-1
Jan. 14	Washington	Tie	3-3 (OT)
Jan. 17	Dallas	Loss	3-2
Jan. 19	Anaheim	Win	5-1
Jan. 20	Los Angeles	Loss	4-1
Jan. 22	Nashville	Win	4-0
Jan. 24	Tampa Bay	Loss	6-2
Jan. 27	Phoenix	Win	2-1
Jan. 28	San Jose	Loss	4-1
Jan. 30	Chicago	Loss	5-3
Feb. 1	Anaheim	Win	6-4
Feb. 3	Los Angeles	Tie	4-4 (Tie)

Feb. 5	St. Louis	Loss	2-1
Feb. 10	Atlanta	Win	5-2
Feb. 11	Vancouver	Win	3-2
Feb. 13	Anaheim	Win	2-1
Feb. 15	Minnesota	Win	2-1
Feb. 19	Montreal	Loss	4-1
Feb. 21	Ottawa	Loss	2-1
Feb. 22	New Jersey	Loss	3-1
Feb. 24	Colorado	Win	2-0
Feb. 26	Detroit	Loss	2-1
Feb. 29	Phoenix	Win	4-2
March 2	St. Louis	Win	4-2
March 3	Detroit	Loss	2-1
March 5	Dallas	Loss	5-1
March 7	Colorado	Win	7-1
March 9	Edmonton	Tie	1-1 (OT)
March 11	Ottawa	Win	4-2
March 13	Nashville	Tie	4-4 (OT)
March 14	St. Louis	Win	3-0
March 16	Detroit	Win	4-1
March 18	Columbus	Win	2-0
March 20	Nashville	Loss	3-1
March 22	Dallas	Loss	4-0
March 24	Phoenix	Win	4-0
March 25	San Jose	Loss	3-2
March 27	Los Angeles	Win	3-2 (OT)
March 31	Phoenix	Win	1-0
April 2	Los Angeles	Win	3-2
April 4	Anaheim	Loss	2-1

Playoffs

April 7	Vancouver	Loss	5-3
April 9	Vancouver	Win	2-1
April 11	Vancouver	Loss	1-2
April 13	Vancouver	Win	4-0
April 15	Vancouver	Win	2-1
April 17	Vancouver	Loss	5-4 (3OT)
April 19	Vancouver	Win	3-2 (OT)
April 22	Detroit	Win	2-1 (OT)
April 24	Detroit	Loss	5-2
April 27	Detroit	Win	3-2
April 29	Detroit	Loss	4-2
May 1	Detroit	Win	1-0
May 3	Detroit	Win	1-0
May 9	San Jose	Win	4-3 (OT)
May 11	San Jose	Win	4-1
May 13	San Jose	Loss	3-0
May 16	San Jose	Loss	4-2
May 17	San Jose	Win	3-0
May 19	San Jose	Win	3-1

Calgary Flames
2003-04
Roster

2003-04 CALGARY FLAMES TEAM ROSTER

No.	Name	Pos	Height	Weight	Born	Birthplace
1	Roman Turek	G	6.04	222 lbs.	05/21/1970	Strak, CZE
2	Mike Commodore	D	6.04	230 lbs	11/07/1979	Ft. Saskatchewan, AB, CAN
3	Denis Gauthier	D	6.02	224 lbs.	10/01/1976	Montreal, QC, CAN
4	Jordan Leopold	D	6.01	205 lbs.	08/03/1980	Golden Valley, MN, USA
5	Steve Montador	D	6.00	211 lbs.	12/21/1979	Vancouver, BC, CAN
7	Chuck Kobasew	RW	6.00	196 lbs.	04/17/1982	Osoyooser, BC, CAN
11	Stephane Yelle	C	6.01	196 lbs.	05/09/1974	Ottawa, ON, CAN
12	Jarome Iginla	RW	6.01	208 lbs.	07/01/1977	Edmonton, AB, CAN
15	Chris Simon	LW	6.03	232 lbs.	01/30/1972	Wawa, ON, CAN
16	Shean Donovan	RW	6.02	209 lbs.	01/22/1975	Timmins, ON, CAN
17	Chris Clark	RW	6.00	200 lbs.	03/08/1976	South Windsor, CT, USA
18	Matthew Lombardi	C	6.00	200 lbs.	03/18/1982	Montreal, QC, CAN
19	Oleg Saprykin	LW	6.01	190 lbs.	02/12/1981	Moscow, RUS
20	Lynn Loyns	C	5.11	205 lbs.	02/22/1981	Naicamt, SK, CAN
21	Andrew Ference	D	5.10	195 lbs.	03/17/1979	Edmonton, AB, CAN
22	Craig Conroy	C	6.02	193 lbs.	09/04/1971	Potsdam, NY, USA
23	Martin Gelinas	LW	5.11	202 lbs.	06/05/1970	Shawnigan, QC, CAN
24	Ville Nieminen	LW	6.01	208 lbs.	04/06/1977	Tampere, FIN
25	Martin Sonnenberg	LW	6.00	197 lbs.	01/23/1978	Wetaskiwin, AB, CAN
26	Marcus Nilson	LW	6.02	195 lbs.	03/01/1978	Balsta, SWE
28	Robyn Regehr	D	6.03	230 lbs.	04/19/1980	Redife, BRA
32	Toni Lydman	D	6.01	204 lbs.	09/25/1977	Lahti, FIN
33	Krzysztof Oliwa	LW	6.05	240 lbs.	04/12/1973	Tychy, POL
34	Miikka Kiprusoff	G	6.02	190 lbs.	10/26/1976	Turku, FIN
37	Dean Mcammond	LW	5.11	198 lbs.	06/15/1973	Grand Cache, AB, CAN
44	Rhett Warrener	D	6.02	215 lbs.	01/27/1976	Shaunavon, SK, CAN

Mike Bynum is one of college football's most successful editors, with best-selling books on the University of Michigan, the national champion Ohio State Buckeyes, Penn State, the University of Alabama, the Tennessee Vols and the University of Texas. He has also edited photo-biographies of Mario Lemieux and Steve Yzerman and his book, *Quest for the Cup: The Detroit Red Wings' 1996-97 Stanley Cup Championship Season*, is one of hockey's all-time bestsellers.

Michelle White is a sports researcher based in Toronto, Ont. She recently co-edited the books, *Greatest Moments in Canada Hockey History*, *The Heritage Classic* and *Greatest Moments in Vancouver Canucks Hockey History*.